Buzz

Buzz

Poets Respond to SWARM

Edited by
Nancy Gifford and Chryss Yost

Gunpowder Press • Santa Barbara
2014

© 2014 by Nancy Gifford and Chryss Yost

Published by Gunpowder Press
David Starkey, Editor
PO Box 60035
Santa Barbara, CA 93160-0035

Back cover: Neal Crosbie

ISBN-13: 978-0-9916651-3-6

www.gunpowderpress.com

ABOUT THE SHORELINE VOICES PROJECT: The Shoreline Voices Project publishes Santa Barbara-area poets writing on a specific theme. We thank Ganna Walska Lotusland, the curators, and the artists of *SWARM: A Collaboration with Bees* for inspiring the poems in this collection.

For the bees

Poems

Hive

Perie Longo "Hive"	13
John Ridland "In the Bee Room"	14
Kurt Brown "Bombing the Swarm"	15
Glenna Luschei "Collecting Nectar"	16
Chryss Yost "Wicked"	17
Gudrun Bortman "Room of Wax"	18
Ron Alexander "Distress Signal"	19
Gabriella Klein "The Honeycomb Conjecture"	20
Wendy Wilder Larsen "Honey Room"	21
Barbara Bates "In an Unfinished Honeycomb: An Old Story"	22
John Ridland "The Bee Room at Lotusland"	23

Buzz

Laure-Anne Bosselaar "Pantoum from a Wax-Tiled Room"	27
Michael Wilds "Daphne"	28
George Yatchisin "Nightingales to Wax"	29
Christine Penko "The Cost of Beauty"	30
Richard Jarrette "Honey for the Women"	31
Barry Spacks "Apollo Plays His Lyre and the Bees Live on Forever"	32
George Yatchisin "After Daphne"	34
Chryss Yost "Gaia's Song"	36
Enid Osborn "Queen of Acacias"	37
Zachary Liebhaber "The Bees"	38
Richard Jarrette "The Godot Tree"	40
Tessa Flanagan "Telling the Keepers"	41
Zachary Liebhaber "The Tale of Daphne and Apollo, Told Again"	42
Barbara Bates "Daphne"	44

Honey

Mary Brown "Of Honey"	47
Marsha de la O "Viento"	48
David Peacock "Six Is Their Number"	50
Luci Janssen "Czarodziejka (Enchantress)"	51
Linda Saccoccio "Daphne's Plea"	52
Peg Quinn "So We Might Know"	56
Diane August "Nectar like Chocolate"	58
Paul J. Willis "Extra Innings"	59
Glenna Luschei "Ganna Walska Rag"	60
Suzanne Frost "Lea and the Sound of Bees"	61
Paul Fericano "Song of the Beeswax"	62
Suzanne Frost "Apollo in the Blue Garden"	64
Tessa Flanagan "The Humming"	66

Dance

Barry Spacks "On Bees and Honey"	69
Enid Osborn "April Swarm"	70
Mary Brown "¹wax \'waks\ n"	71
Michael Wilds "The Good Sisters"	72
Luci Janssen "Beescape"	73
RBS "The eeriness lies in the absence"	74
John Elliot "The Bee as Artist"	78
Frances Davis "Last Dance"	80
Pamela Davis "Queen"	82
Susan Chiavelli "Blue Honey"	83
John Elliot "A True Account of an Extraordinary Conversation with a Bee in Lotusland"	84

Curators' Note

In Spring 2013, the magical pink walls of the fantastical garden Ganna Walska Lotusland in Montecito, California, became a frame for "SWARM: A Collaboration with Bees." SWARM encouraged contemporary artists to explore and expose the plight of the honeybee and the vagaries of the bee colony collapse disorder. Poets from Santa Barbara were invited to revel in the intensity of artistic expression. *Buzz: Poets Respond to Swarm* is the product of their direct interactions with the art.

As part of the SWARM exhibit, Canadian artist Penelope Stewart spent a month in residence at Lotusland. Stewart tiled an entire room with 1000 pounds of beeswax cast into lotus pods, succulent plants, and architectural details from Lotusland itself. Her Daphne room infused SWARM with the fragrance of honeycomb.

Many of the poets wrote about the sensory and emotional overload of being inside the Daphne chamber. Others were inspired by the allegory of Daphne, the beauty of the Lotusland gardens, or the behavior of the bees themselves. The colorful life of Ganna Walska, the opera singer who created Lotusland's eccentric gardens, was a muse throughout.

These poems are about bees and their habits in our culture but viewed through the intensified lens of dramatic artistic expression.

Nancy Gifford, Guest Curator
Gwen Stauffer, Executive Director, Ganna Walska Lotusland

HIVE

Hive

"If the bee disappeared off the surface of the globe, then man would only have four years of life left. No more bees, no more pollination, no more plants..."
—*Albert Einstein*

        Have we like the bee
      arrived in heaven after all,
    here every sweet thing sealed
   from harm in wax, honey's smell
dispelling any desire but swarm with
our kind in a soul dance, wings aflame
at the Queen's call, to please the Queen
who keeps life humming along—we must
succumb or else the world becomes a flimsy
thing, gone in a whim, bellies bulged after miles
flown combing the earth, our task to dust off our
wings, bestir nature's splurge to begin again, recall
the myth—nymph's shun of one god for the whole,
O the drone of our song is dirge, this aureate womb
silk to the touch we finger and swoon ... tiles coupled
with succulent heads, lotus pod upon pod and wrought
knob after knob, a warning time is now to turn and soon.

In the Bee Room

Not understanding what we see as beauty—
        A bee's eye magnified a thousand-fold
        And littered with gigantic grains of gold—
Pollen that's standing by to do its duty:

To pollinate; and spike our allergy chart.
        Why do we sneeze and choke at what they give?
        Why do we kill what's there to help us live?
We've lost our place in the book we knew by heart

Before we wrote our own books. We're misreading.
        What is a bee-sting but a sharp reminder
        That other kingdoms, crueler and kinder,
Reign all around us, in us, onward leading,

Pleading with us to keep them living free?
Thus we call lovely the huge eye of a bee.

Bombing the Swarm

This swarm of bees was hanging
from the branch of a tall tree,
a writhing mass that clung together
and swung down like a black bell.

One of the boys, can't remember who,
picked up an apple—it was late August—
51 or 52—and hurled it into the nest:
it came apart in hunks, like a skull exploding,

then recomposed; but we kept hurling apples
and the swarm kept flying apart, flying together,
replay of a bullet entering a man's brain.
Looking back, I realize we couldn't stop,

neither could the bees, we had this frenzy.
That's when I learned how dangerous
I was—so that now when I walk in a field,
my shadow makes crickets hush

and birds fly away in alarm.

Collecting Nectar

The bees who circle the mask of the bee keeper
when he transports them to the ranch

strive for their zenith.   The lotus, too, that blooms from stagnant
waters. The bees prefer the lotus and the lavender

to avocado but they pollinate the blossoms and I collect
the nectar. No fear. A thrill to take part in creation.

Bearing fruit is the fulfillment of the Kingdom.
Daphne turns the doorknob and becomes a laurel.

How fragrant and ripe the grove when I collect the nectar

Still it must all come down, life in its dismantling.
Tiles of beeswax return to vat.

Death seeks metamorphosis, too. We bloom, bear fruit,
die and resurrect as tree or insect.

It must all come down
Into the empty, open patio. We start again with swarm.

Wicked

You are the swarm gathering force, collecting
and constructing. I feel the walls rise, warming, fragrant.
The wind stills. What need have we for windows?
This desire, the need of blossoms to be kissed,
for pollen mulled in the mouth like a poem
to be shaped into lotus pods, to be filled with seed,
to open in heat. Lucky wick, surrounded by softening
wax, sweet with the breath of bees.

Room of Wax

Palmitate, oleate esters—
beeswax composition—
these words do not speak of amber,
saffron and gold, not the balm
of these redolent walls,
nor how they soothe me

to the river-land back home,
orchards tucked in the shelter of dikes,
gnarled apple trees
glazed pink and white,
hours dozy with the thrum of bees;

back to my Pennsylvania kitchen
sucking honey from dripping combs,
taste of the summer meadow,
blue bells and clover.
Pale flecks of wax
cling to my lips like torn petals, bees,
besotted, tumble in to kiss them away.

Distress Signal

within the hive
walls sprout sedum, curling
leaves, lotus pods
doorknobs

waxy writing on the wall
bees sculpt a warning

The Honeycomb Conjecture

If a bee is busy, too busy
to feel woe. Or the absence
of pollen, which is to say, lonely.
I would lie with you
in the open road.
As a bee's light
we are a premise untested.
Some forces act upon the nucleus
while others extend.
Massless particles, messengers.
Inside us
lives a colony of space.
In catacombs of wax
grief can be
both fungus and virus.
The holes regret fills.
Unborn, unwritten,
unmet, unsaid.
Nectar adhering
to static and fuzz.
Hive collapse is nearly.
We are losing our ability
to navigate home.

Honey Room

A whole room of beeswax—a smooth skin
inviting you in, tiles in tones of butterscotch
and amber, humming gold and warmth

a skin molded, embosed with lotus,
luring caramel and sweet moan,
love makings in the afternoon

breathing fragrance in the scented air
tempting you to linger in that room
not wanting to get out of bed

staying on in the morning
under the drowsy covers
just a little longer

the scented time says *ambrosia*
you can't be drunk enough
I am the jewel at the heart of the lotus

breathe in the sweetness
open like the flower for the bee
who came on heavy wings to drink

honeycomb, my soul's home
here I can stay, a place to say *round*
to say *O*, to say *gold*
to say *hold*.

In an Unfinished Honeycomb: An Old Story

As lichen on a rock spreads, so you grow
into love on the lap of your mother til—
smothering her presence you burst aglow
into green adolescence. Seldom still,
you run before the bulls, climb peaks, trade in
dreams to feed your striving. Oh saboteur
of mild, homespun days! Consider now
the work of bees, how they nourish our lusting
yet protect our prey. Just as browning leaves
feed the bulbs of flowers long past their bloom,
the humble bee waxes the circle, curbs
the excesses of lovers willing to defer
to the queen who fills wellsprings
with the only breath that can move her wings.

The Bee Room at Lotusland

After W. B. Yeats, "The Lake Isle of Innisfree"

I will arise and go now, and go to Lotusland,
With thirty poets standing, as in Qin's Imperial Tomb,
Like terra cotta soldiers armed with pen and pad in hand,
Reporting for duty in the beeswax room.

And I shall eat some cheese there, with white wine—just a sip:
I'm driving—pouring from the bottle, where the spirit sings
Of Madame Ganna Walska, who would join our fellowship,
Were she not a ghost on gold bee wings.

I will arise and go now, not to miss my stroke of luck,
For I hear the bees a-humming with low sounds inside the hive,
While I wander by the lotus pond with its solitary duck.
I hear them even as I leave and drive.

BUZZ

Pantoum from a Wax-Tiled Room

And so the bees keep coming to the lotus garden.
And so the bees came to gather in the laurel's limbs.
And at dusk—from a gold and wax-tiled room—heard
Daphne's call. How she called, how she called.

And so the bees came to gather in the laurel's limbs.
So many swarms gone, but a few still hearing
Daphne's call. How she called, how she called
from each anther and stigma, each succulent's curl.

So many swarms gone, but a few still hearing
that cry from the threshold and honeyed walls,
from each anther and stigma, each succulent's curl.
Then the owl, the children and even a griffin heard

that cry from the threshold and honeyed walls,
they stopped, listened, their hearts beat wilder.
Then the owl, the children and even a griffin heard
Daphne sing now—she sang: it was no longer a call.

They stopped, listened, their hearts beat wilder
and at dusk—from a gold and wax-tiled room—heard
Daphne sing now—she sang: it was no longer a call.
And so the bees keep coming to the lotus garden.

Daphne

So, wax it lines the alcove and it breathes
its honey-colored scent into the air
translucent gold upon the wall it sheathes.

Each pilgrim come is painfully aware
the candlesticks are empty of their lights,
the doorknobs fit no hands and lead nowhere,

still, at this doorless threshold an insight:
the dead-end path we've followed to this wall,
a mirror, in which we recognize the blight

that withers hope and leads to our downfall
is us. This nectar dazzles as it dooms,
with its persistent sweetness it forestalls

our wistful recognition that the tomb
we stand in is the triumph of the bees,
and all of this engendered by a room:

Once Daphne ran to her fate as do we.
Love chased her, and we stand before her frieze,
hoping, when gone, to rise again as trees.

Nightingales to Wax

Antiquity is too many men after too many women,
with little woo about it, at least till the troubadours,
who made love sweet merely for their art's sake, Provençal
rhyming heart, love, flower, and so they simply sang along.
Till then the repeated stories were of force, of chase, of furious fate.
Change the only escape. And escape does not mean grace:
Mulberries stain vermilion for love-struck Thisbe,
Arachne edges her eight legs into all our darkest nights,
Myyrha, already a fabulously fragrant tree, gives birth to Adonis.
How rarely we recall beauty and desire had such beginnings.
Poor Philomela raped and her tongue cut to silence her
cry of her crimes, ends up the nightingale, a revenge odd
in the real world where female nightingales have no song.
And poor Daphne, to save her from Apollo's Cupid-induced love
Gaia turns her into a laurel, her leaves a symbol of others' victories.
This is the way we make the sorrowful, silent bird sing,
this is the way the pursued maiden buds into everlasting beauty,
this is the way we take the sting of mean from meaning,
this is the way we discover what metaphor is for.

The Cost of Beauty

They wanted their freedom, women. Beautiful.

    Unable to elude Apollo's reach Daphne wills her feet take root.
        Her arms become a manyness, shelter teeming
          hives of bees. Alone, she contemplates stars
            circling her Laurel canopy.

                Ganna flees—
            six marriages brief as bees—

            wanders half a lifetime—
    every coupling a loss until she wills her feet take root,
her garden, teeming with life, a consolation for barren arms.

            The wind becomes Daphne's voice.
              Ganna's garden her choir.

                  *

    Rooted for eternity, Daphne lives, her fine greenery woven
        into wreaths, her beauty everlasting.

                Death captures Ganna

        yet her garden thrives, season to season
   retelling the story of a woman who spent to her last on beauty

                        beauty, on beauty.

Honey for the Women

Earth wins its argument again.
I sit beneath a tree to rest, filled with living
like a worm full of dirt, and I Euripides
about the women I've known.

My fingers find a crusty dead bee in the grass,
weightless, more profound than the Song of Solomon.
Inside its husk, a hundred million years of nectar dances,
flowers of the world and the world's sweetness.

But I robbed the tree of a kernel of food
by picking it up and so I put it down.

If I never get up and no one finds me,
will bees make a hive of my body as in Samson's lion
and honey, from alfalfa and sage,
next spring?

Apollo Plays His Lyre and the Bees Live on Forever

Our deepest desire is to serve, transcend,
heal the sick bees, protect fleeing maidens,

so Daphne stays chaste, become a bay laurel,
by myth made safe from the God's pursuit.

She'd prayed for the chance to be saved from her beauty
though Phoebus himself aspired as her lover.

Her leaves bewreathe artists with ultimate praise,
Laureate Makers unwearied by Time.

While humans forge art and bees craft honey
high myth provides meanings that never fade.

In art the dear bees will live on forever;
the God sing unceasing love to his maiden.

*

Life depends upon carnal longing.
It's *meant* in us, our heat, our questing,

but time-bound desire pursues grander meanings,
eternal life through the grace of art.

The artist is bee to process, surviving
loss in a stir toward triumphant work.

    Where is the jewel?
      In the lotus.

    The root of the lotus?
      Deep in the pond's mud.

    Our ultimate nature?
      Quick: speak your answer!

After Daphne

It begins with
        a halo of buzz
                about her cauldron
no ingredient
        odder than wax
                of bees warming
waiting for molds
        like Walska shaping
                nature into what she
wanted nature to be
        perhaps a garden
                edited only to blue
or masses of euphorbias
        despite their name weeping
                rising returning to earth
as bees called back
        to wax not theirs
                as if owning means
anything when it's beauty
        you can smell
                home you can taste
this not quite room
        three walls we stare
                into like a sepia stage
waiting for what
        must begin again
                lotus pods free of seeds

so useless and gorgeous
        something we can hope
                is the before we waited for
a stinging kiss of
        many myths and Ovid
                a busy midwife birthing
none less so than
        we are what
                we leave behind
a belief we need
        as badly as the bee
                knowing only the geometry
of six-sides, of so much
        sweet chewed down
                to wax to walls
to the order
        of a life too short
               to leave complaint room

Gaia's Song

All I am is made to tend the future
for you, daughter. I travel, only gather
and retrieve, land on and abandon.
Remember me as mother when you leave.

Each day as morning dries to heat I lift
my frame against the wind, as flight
is what you need and I need give.
Remember me as mother when you fly.

All I am is charm to save you, daughter,
weak magic just like water in the way
like wishing wicked footsteps pass you by.
Remember me as mother when you hide.

I wish you untouched, irresistible girl,
with roots that will protect you, leaves
glorious, reaching away from this world.
Remember me as mother when you rise.

Queen of Acacias

The waxmakers brought her to this gaping tree
They nursed her fever with powdered acacia

chucked their droplets between her jaws
She convulsed

and when she awoke from her dream of flight
she was a slave in a labyrinth of cribs

They multiply daily
She suffocates in velvet

Sly maids bring her rich food
and gossip from the lost world

When she panics, the sycophants
pet her face, she could die

What madness it was to dance
with the poets and their violas

Those rare boys will drag their circles
in the first dust

while she is heavy with heat
drugged and surrounded

taking one step, one step, one step

The Bees

Patches of color, in open sun,
Against the rocky ground,

The flowers draw the bees in—
The foragers zig-zagging

About from spot to spot,
According to internal maps

That seem to change and realign
Faster than the workings of the human mind.

The ancients had a sense of this:
Jonathan dipped his staff

Into the honey comb,
"And his eyes were bright."

Apollo's oracle took honey
That she might recite her words

And so confuse,
With rhyme and cryptic images,

Her supplicants already confused:
Men see the things they wish to see.

The bee, old symbol of eternal life,
Moves from shape to shape,

And sign to sign—sees forward,
Deeply, into light.

The Godot Tree

> *How sad the tree was destroyed.*
> *The tree at the Odéon was destroyed in sixty-eight.*
> *Giacometti's tree, the Godot tree.*
> —Samuel Beckett

Vultures flap to roosts and shut their eyes.
I brace for the wild barking and suddenly forgetful frogs.

The silhouette of a voice, backlit by silence,
summons me to namelessness.

Old dreams swim in the blood, coyotes
harrow Orion's dogs.

Beckett and Giacometti worked long on the Godot tree—
a starved tree, ridiculous, useless

for a hanging, Giacometti's dog couldn't piss on it;
a post-Death Camp tree, postmodern,

post-bees.

Telling the Keepers

Bees of paradise were white,
but when we followed you
to this place, we turned brown
and brown we stay with you.
We mine the flower caverns
dusted in pollen's gold,
seeing with honeycomb eyes
the honeycomb imprint
of land-dwelling life.
Our fates are bound together
in honey, mead, and death.
Tell us of births and weddings,
baptize the babes with honey,
honey the lips of the bride,
and wait at the door with honey.
Our wax will light your way.
We will fly through your house,
swarm to bring good luck.
We'll bless your hand with gold,
bless your head with fortune,
our amber benediction.
Speak to us of loss,
fresh in your Sunday suit,
tie black crepe upon the hive.
Tell us what we must know.
We hum the sacred hymn,
dance the holy steps
that guide the new-freed soul
safely to the lotus land.

The Tale of Daphne and Apollo, Told Again

Even Apollo, the Lord of Light,
Was not immune to Love's unswerving arrow.
Heart molten with desire, transformed by love,
(And slave to it) he sings to her:

"Daphne, best of river maidens,
The wilderness is rough,
The thorns will tear your flesh,
Beauty is my song, eloquence, my crown.
I see past, present, and ..."

This music, so full of his intent,
Too much for her to bear (still a child),
Drives Daphne away—not into the wild,
But to the gardens of Arcadia:
The quiet pillars, paths, and springs,
Ancient land of ancient gods,
Beside a running stream.

To her father, old spirit of that place,
She cries:
"Protect me from Apollo's care!"
Then stops, and thinks, and turns her mind
Inward (and her back to fate—
An impulse just as old as love)

Until her thoughts and matter become one.
Blossoms spring from fingertips,
Her limbs grow hard and ramify,
Up and out, against the clear, blue sky.
Her feet extend and root into the earth.

Apollo, Lord of Light, and Poetry, finds her,
Her transformation just complete,
Still trembling from the force of it,
The tremors moving out in waves, from trunk
To furthest branch, then past each fine, leaf tip:

Across the narrow borderline,
Shining—taut as a well-tuned string—
That lies along the edge of things.

Daphne

The bee guards saw her first (Apollo
hard upon her) and ordered the bark
of the old hollow tree they called home,
to open. She ran in and embraced
the hive with her fading body, and while
the workers out among the flowers hummed
unaware, the indolent queen paused
in her begetting to order the drones
to anoint the new virgin wood with
her royal jelly. Never was a lovelier
tree so made evergreen, and though Apollo
watched in dismay and grief, he wove
her sweet foliage into a crown—a Laurel
to honor all poets and musicians.

Honey

Of Honey

Collect me from nectar,
you field bee of flattery,
sweetheart of hexagonal,
vexation of swarm.

Honeycomb me; I will
flower you.

Viento

Did I mention I'm afraid of the dark?
>> The wind too: *Vientophobia*,
> my doctor calls it. Sets me on edge.

>> All the little hairs on my forearms
>>> trilling upward. That night
> a gale swept through, and a honey bee
>>> buzzed free, lumbering in my kitchen,

wind-rocked darkness, the bee must have
> been whistled down and scrabbled
through the fan housing.

>> She rose by instinct, an older
>>> female sent out to forage
in the fields of the realm, I like to say—
>>> always wished I was one of them,

old-woman-ecstatic lipping goblets
> on the trumpet vine,
anyway she's rising toward stovelight

>> when her thorax touches the flood—
>>> living flesh against diode sizzles-
down hard, thrown to the floor by force,
>> no telling if light ate the filaments

of her wings, still carrying treasure for the hive,
>   *oro blando*, velvety damp
> morsels of pollen. *And where art thou now,*

>   *O Queen?* Somewhere close by, bringing forth
>   eggs? Male and female she makes
> them, opens the ductile to her sac of sperm,
>   fertile and infertile she forms them

in their golden cells. And her daughters shape the waxen
>   cakes, her sisters build the combs,
> and the old ones beat their wings and tremble

>   in the fields. Now the night careens
>   toward me in the gyre of the wind,
> now the stunned elder sister is laid on alien ground,
>   *Your servant, Majesty, alone in the dark*

Six Is Their Number

Bees have six legs.
Some bees have six bands of black on their abdomen.
These are facts.
Facts are not poetry.
When I find facts in my poems,
I am disappointed in the poem.
My friend Robert, calls this binary thinking.

The bees create their hives based on a hexagon.
Six sides of each cylindrical cell.
I am interested in the flat plane of the cells.
Humans use the straight line, the flat plane, and the cube for design.

This is a key that connects our society to the bees.

I watch the bees and see their six obsessions with industry,
communication, productivity, procreation, building and society.

This thought,
is a poem.

Czarodziejka (Enchantress)

she gathers her skirts laced with gold
sets out on dewy morn
hums an aria as she flits
from perfumed bowers to home

she shakes her laden petticoats
dusts the floor with gilded nectar
pirouettes 'til it gleams in golden lustre
claps to see such aureate splendor

what ambered alchemy is this
that lines her ambrosial chambers
such succulent delights her just rewards
borne by her apian merry mettle

she carries on from dawn to dusk
from work to reverie
while wealth abounds in her garden
precious elixir flows through her being

Daphne's Plea

Imagine, if you would
A static immovable feast
Dry and lifeless
A place of no flavor
devoid of scent
caving and crumbling
into fine decay
dust of a civilization
If you could
If you would
dare to imagine
the horror
the lifeless state
of being without
the diversity
we have come to
take, as normal
everyday, quotidian
the varied patterns and shapes
Such as Ganna's succulent garden
displays, her dense jungle of cycads, palms
and cacti worlds
the fragrance of jasmine or orange blossoms
sweetening Spring
the taste of honey
on the tongue
in your tea
the fragrance and
purification that

Daphne's bees wax tile
room surrounds you
in a sanctuary of
remembrance
of paradise
freedom
stability
grace in flight
of bees,
Daphne
protecting and preserving
feminine pools
of water
that reflect our
universe
the cycles of
organic restoration and regeneration
You cannot do without
You will not even imagine
for you like Ganna or Daphne
will not compromise
will not sacrifice
a world of bees
pollination
flowers, food,
soulful sustenance
You will not
for yourself nor
for generations to be

let the bees die
Unimaginable
Unforgivable
would be your
true grit
bound to your
vision like these
tiles of bees wax ornaments
that echo passion
rhythm, dreams of yesterday and
endless tomorrows
Pineapple fruit fertility
Repetition in patterns
a bee's hive
collaborating for the benefit
of the swarm
the queen
the fruit of life
Its nectar our assurance of
survival
You will establish
the order, balance and diversity
That is in your own DNA
in harmony with divine
echoes in every living plant and creature
on this swirling blue planet
You will and you must
See the reflection
the beauty
bees sustain

to secure your
beating heart
your breathing pulse
your hunger for beauty
Stand tall as the tree
of life
whether Daphne or Ganna
you turn your attention
to the gift that requires
your care-taking
Paring it back
to respect

So We Might Know

Though shaded gardens
stretch before me
I sit on a bench,
lower my head and thank
mysterious forces,
creators of kingdoms
I have entered,
where artists scrape
with razor blades
or photograph
with such precision

I nibble edges
of a universe that resides
in antenna, hinges, eyes,
artists who provide
a bee's view.

Praise the minds
that hear the call
to lower cameras
into hexagons
so we might know
the dance
as best we can
and having entered in

I ask you, please,
let us heed such steps
and dance,
and dance
through this world
and the next.

Nectar like Chocolate

Lured to cherry blossom's
tender magenta center
Plunge my proboscis
into moistness
Sucking luscious
stirs me dizzy

Crave tastes of this lenten rose
you unbearable delicacy
I lick your lush yellow core
Oh, shimmer slippery
nectar drops

Soft poppy, do spread me
with yellow pollen
Coat my gold and black body
head and legs—the tip
of my barbed stinger

Filled, I fly into the vibration
our hive—the drum, the hum
the honey vapors
Wings beating—fanning
Trembling, I begin the waggle
the tell of the find
Our queen's scented pheromones
weaving, waving
yes, completely entrancing

Extra Innings

From a shaky scaffold rising out of the poison oak,
a pair of men are tearing off
the back of our redwood baseball stands.

Who would have guessed it?
Between the boards, row on row of honeycombs,
packed in like a visiting team in brown and saffron uniforms.

All these years a sweetness
building at our backs, a hidden infield
of play, the score kept in numberless columns

by so many runs home. Here was a game
never called on account of darkness,
only halted by too much light.

Ganna Walska Rag

Oh Ganna, how we love ya.
Your stand of Clivia bright,
we stride to your door, on to the Daphne room.
Pursued by Apollo, Daphne blossomed into a laurel tree.
Hounded by music critics, you turned into an icon,

Oh Ganna of the Clivia,
inspire us
Nothing could get you down.

You remember Clive of India, founder of the British Empire
who brought Clivia nobilis from Swaziland. No bulbs, no seed,
but he transplanted it. You upon the stage in your grandeur.
They said you had no voice, but your reverberations draw
the bees to us. Your music escapes from sound.

Oh Ganna of the Lotus,
open us.
Your music escapes from sound.
Nothing can get you down.

Oh Ganna, how we love ya
and your excess. What a blessing your sixth husband brought
you to the sacred Lotus, Nelumba nucifera, and you bloom
as the Lotus, out of mess. Penelope through her beeswax vat
opened the door to you. You opened the door for us.

Lea and the Sound of Bees

> *una apis, nulla apis (One bee is no bee.)*
> —*Proverb*
> *For my gardener-friend, Lea*

An evolutionary miracle, this
artist flyer, this political sculptor of honeycomb
harvest gardens, you who dip into flowers

then instantly begin
to make dinner in your honey-sac
with the nectar you've found.

Your multiplicity of sounds astonish even more,
the pipe of the virgin queen
before you've first left your cell,

or the warble of the nurse-bee
if you produce more milk than us larva can drink,
or the hiss while you're working, if something knocks

on our colony's wall. Bees are like you, Lea,
the truest givers of the world
community first, faithful friend to your adoring hive.

Forever and always you
forage and plunder our heart's honey
with your blithesome, boundless buzz.

Song of the Beeswax

I.

sing the songing and the longing and belonging of the bees
        of the bee's eye, bee's eye, bee's eye bees
        of the bee's eye view of the bee's eye bees
and the buzz of the buzzing of the buzzing of the bees

be the busy of a bumble and as busy as a bee
        as the busy in the bumble is the busy in the bee
        and the busy as a busy is as busy as a bee
is as busy as a bumble as a bumble is a bee

II.

see the seeing and believing and the being of the bees
        and the bees, and the bees, and the bees in the bees
        and the bees and the birds and the birds and the bees
and the bees in the bonnet and the bonnet in the bees

be the bee in the bees in the knees of the bees
        and the bees in the flowers and the flowers in the bees
        see the bees in the trees and the trees in the bees
and the bees in the honey and the honey in the bees

III.

be the drumming and the coming and the humming of the bees
      of the bees of the bees of the bees of the bees
      all the telling and the belling and the spelling of the bees
and the moaning and the groaning and the droning of the bees

sing the songing and the longing and belonging of the bees
      of the bee's eye, bee's eye, bee's eye bees
      of the bee's eye view of the bee's eye bees
and the buzz of the buzzing of the buzzing of the bees

Apollo in the Blue Garden

Non Noblis (Not for Ourselves)

The longer you dance, my love,
the further away you are.
Your waggle and buzz in our newly waxened boudoir

point us where the sun and nectar are.
Divine my honey, my sweet queen bee,
you who drink only the purest water and share your garden

with us all. Yes, yes, I will save your bees,
my mother of thousands, my "enemy of average"
but for once, let the mortals fertilize their own crops!

Though you won't. For you
there's always room at the top,
even for me, your love-drunk, all-alleviating God of arias.

I haven't felt your sting, Ganna dear,
that brink of sinking into Narcissus's pool.
For no splintered, mourning soul

would I lavish my fortunes and favor.
You corralled me to your columnar cactus grove,
then drew me to your white-bottomed pond

adorned with Aphrodite shell.
Without protest, you wear my abalone well.
Guided by astrology's ancient clock,

I bask in your Lotusland touch
with no fear. Just you and I are here, my dear,
among these Elysian hedges, let us

caress again and again under the lemon arbor?
You have me in the Mexican blue palm
of your Chilean wine hand. Through your atlas

cedar hair Apollo runs his hands.
Only your aloe from Madagascar
will soothe my burning, insatiable heart!

The Humming

As I descend into the valley,
the air is humming,
low, around my feet
where scrubby little flowers huddle.
I look for bees, see none.
The valley fills with humming,
branches of trees are humming.
I look for hives or brown beards
of bees, swarming,
but there are none.
And yet each leaf is vibrating,
the stones in the creek
and the rippling surface,
the sandstone boulders
rising sentinel on the hillside,
the air, heavy and enveloping,
all humming around me,
the hum of petals and bark,
of dust and water, sun and rock.
My cells, my honeycomb cells,
are full of the sweetness of humming,
the humming always with me,
never heard before.

DANCE

On Bees and Honey

Scientists claim that bees do not dance
(as once was thought) directing their sisters
to fields of choice flowers ... but I say they do;

the bees still left us, I say they dance
displaying by movement the way to go
to gather up nectar for making honey.

*

Sprites of Spring on the balance-bars
bounce like lambs in the April fields
while plum blossoms flirt with their bees.

Rilke declares us "bees of the invisible."
Glorious, doing our work, to emerge
covered with such pollen.

April Swarm

Like a movie of raindrops played backward
the bees fall up into the cactus tree
and make a muscle on the branch

A thousand golden bodies
condense, mold quickly
into the shape of a mustard jar
or a human heart
that you could cup your hands around
if you believed.

¹wax \'waks\ n

: akin to

        bees and is

  the honeycomb   yellow

esters   acids

    called also

origin

      : a solid   : a liquid

: some-

thing   soft,   read y

The Good Sisters

These bees are nuns, celibate, fierce, identically attired.
Their convent, abuzz with news of work undone,
almost trembles with the hum of ceaseless prayer.

Their cloister air (as in all holy places) is heavy laden
with the scent of wax and flowers, of sanctity and grace.
Here are no idle hands to do the devil's work.

Their simple Kirk set to God's business--the gospel of life;
body and soul. They glow with ardor, spreading their good news
through all our countrysides—Hosanna! Awake!

The sisters share no ache of languor; there are no empty hours:
What fails must be perpetually re-knit, and the light of life must ever be re-lit.

Beescape

bespectacled bees
see perspectively
cartography topography
quite skeptically

The eeriness lies in the absence

The eeriness lies in the absence
and like the deepest of subversions
All that is being modified
is announced casually, without concern
as if only a change in the direction
of a gentle breeze
Surely an innocuous development
in the midst of so much progress for the greater good
as if disappearance was the benign foreshadowing
of an era of peace and calm.

Before an earthquake
cattle will lie down without a sound
So the silence begins to prevail
like a soothing blanket dropped over a feverish child
As one penetrates through the border copse
into the deeper throes of our forest primeval,
one can hear that the thrumming
of our globe's nervous systems
is diminishing
Where are the little heralds of our basic health
and honey'd goodness?
Listen! The smallest sounds of well-being are being vanquished
Those industrious airborne riders, the engineers of crop diversity,
not without their bite and sting to protect their queen,
are disappearing.

This is the most insidious fascism
proclaimed as the march of brilliant evolution,
Technological supremacy of mankind
in triumphant procession,

As the natural order is re-arranged,
audited, even patented for a remunerative future
to benefit all manners of masters of life.

But between heaven and earth
there is a message from these smallest minions of space
And the message is slipping between the molecules
escaping our spectrum
Our ears are being slowly shattered
by a withdrawal and the wax
of our hearing loss builds up
Society experiences a widespread tinnitus,
a background noise of binary registry
The world-wide transactions 24/7
of money, profits and loss, flowing
faster than the speed of light
through space and the Internet web of Indra
None of this will reproduce what is being lost.

It is not the buzzing of health by any means,
But the aggravated pump of too much adrenaline, anxiety,
caffeine and cortisol
Our systems inside and out are being assaulted
by the endless march of greed and accumulation
and gluttony for false sweetness.

Despite the dismal vision of fearful religions
women and men and creatures of no creator
are born noble, even brave
We walk upright, poised for more than just survival
It is dignity inherent, full of grace and grit

We begin as one with breath
and body and mind are synchronized
by simple appreciation of life
We breathe to live, and smile and cry to love.
Birds sing, flowers blossom, children play,
winds blow without origin, and ocean waves roll
and every form of being moves and echoes,
sharing the common heartbeat of existence.

But until a point has been reached,
where there may be no return,
we struggle with straw dogs
A shift has occurred—
some changes happen in space not time
And in the air around us
a sound has stopped.

It is connected by a fragile thread
to beauty and joys and the sugar of life,
to the fruition of plants and nuts we eat
Yet, stunned, deprived of our own invisible pollination
by the smells and vibrations of nearby swarms,
we cease to sway to the beat of the blood in our veins
The instinct to invent another dance step
is crippled by so many versions
of corporate turf toe and fasciitis of ambition
Our suppleness turns rigid while
we are still planting conquering flags
We copyright genetics and try to patent nature.

How monstrous and deluded
is all of our labeling
The name of the thing is not the thing
but a deception to afford us ownership
But we can't take away what we didn't give.

Our grins turn crooked and wooden
and there is no more drumming
of fingers or footbeats
The humming has all been withdrawn
The crops and wild life and unnamed rhythms
that carry us through our profound and brilliant glories
are losing their strength
We need the royal jelly, not modified foods.

We long for the birth of music and bounce,
the surging of inner intuitions and tempos
in step with laughter and passion
Life is sweet and ever meant to be
in taste, in touch, in sex, in dreams,
in sleep, and always in waking
We yearn to breathe in the elements and smells
of "trees and greenery and so on"
And no amount of chemicals and scientific genius
will suffice to hold our attention or
inspire us to hold our breath.

No, real inspiration leads to real expiration,
to the circling cycle of in and out, like a bellows
that fans the flames of healthy arrogance
and healthy lust and tender loving kindness
Our passions must play, wisdom must breathe
We must stay close with all we might be
Look and listen, for the humming and buzzing—
They are sweetness and light, they are part of who we are
They are dying to be heard.

The Bee as Artist

She leaves the swarm to travel alone,
testing the spiral loop of consciousness,
exploring the known and unknown.
It might appear she visits only those
flowers which have been exploited
before, tasting the familiar. But what
seems constant to the ancient flora
is, in reality, perusing the known with
a magic eye. She sees differently the
ultraviolet paths leading down the
floral tube, and senses volatiles in marks
of bees which passed before. Sampling,
she learns clovers are easy and sage
amusing, a portal rocking in the wind
like a shaking walkway in a fun house.
But then, a zygomorphic challenge—
she tugs at a new flower form and argues
with herself: is this where she should bee?

Nectar filled and legs adorned with
pollen, she returns to the swarm.
There, others dance and jive, buzz
and nudge the same old dance, a dance
of comfort when she was young but
now passé. She leaves the swarm
with sharpened eye, spends hours
at her task, a floral form untested

by bees her kind. While she works
she knows the angry bee hive dance
awaits, drones and workers both, their
shouts when she appears with pollen
new, with nectar of a different brew—
how they will turn, circle round, resume
their native dance and wish the world remain
the same. In solitude, and sure, her voice
and vision rise in gold-leaf dream and
shower on this flower in its new-born gleam.

Last Dance

Listen sisters, watch me dance
observe my circle
the refraction of light—there

on the sun's right side
beyond the clover patch
that was sheared

See the full baskets I bring,
pollen for the dwindling hive
taste the nectar on my tongue

See how dizzily I spin
the distance and the markers
watch me dance

Beyond the lacuna where
the clover was; those sweet heads
will come again, sisters—

what is riven can be mended—
past the foxglove with its honey
spots and the purple salvia

the starry borage where the light
shines fully round,
the apple tree is pushing

out pale buds, the heart
of every nectar-scented bloom
newly printed for our eyes

Watch me dance
you sisters who survive
above the soft and bumbled

bodies windrowed
below the hive—
what is riven can be mended

Far from here the white
apple blossoms tremble
for the touch of our tongues

Queen

Look how her attendants tremble to serve! Groomed, fed
in an amber womb, she dreams not of them, but an April morning

she flew away, briefly free, from her room of wax. Too fast
the sky grew black with pursuers drunk on her musk. They burrowed

her body, spent their sex. She beat loose, rose once more. In the high silence
her eye compounded ovals, waterways, wildflowers—

space. Clarity. What tiny general ordered
her back? Enthroned, choked in gold, she spills forth eggs, two

thousand today, two thousand tomorrow. For five years. Seven. Workers bump
back and forth, their wings dusted with the forsaken world. They bear lotus,

lavender, attar of roses. Flightless, thick, she drowses in the hum.
Called back by dream, she lifts her head, crawls on trampled wing toward the other

realm she'd known. One part sky. One of brook. Bells of open-throated petals.

Blue Honey

Blue honey tastes like sorrow
Old dad wonders where the bees have gone
He touches the empty hive and sighs
Wild cherry dreams of bursting fruit

Old dad wonders where the bees have gone
They've gone to Lotus Land
Wild cherry dreams of bursting fruit
The echium sings its prideful song

They've gone to Lotus Land
Bees swarm the cottage door
The echium sings its prideful song
Poets journey to the story

Blue honey tastes like sorrow
Bees swarm the cottage door
Poets journey to the story
We touch the empty hive and sigh

A True Account of an Extraordinary Conversation with a Bee in Lotusland

The moon reluctantly moved in place, light
rippled from the silver bowls of abalone shells.
How good it was! A luminous pool silent and
serene ... then a buzz shot by, nicking my ear.

Bee! I spoke angrily. It's night! What are you doing?

The bee, with the graceful curves of bee calligraphy,
scrolled B – U – Z – Z above the water's slate.

Can't you see I'm enjoying the quiet, I protested,
the moon, pool, the peace of this Japanese garden?

She hovered in front of me, her legs dangling
as if to enter the lip of a purple sage. Yet nectar,
or teaching me the art of sting, wasn't her concern.
It's so like you! she huffed, assuming only you
can appreciate a garden or a pool! The truth
is: all who gaze are owners.

Hah! I snorted. You think by merely looking
I own this place?

Ignorant fool, of course you do! Who can
rob you of what you see as long as you
remember? She flew a figure eight & returned.
Of course, with multiple eyes I enjoy this garden
a thousandfold, including wavelengths and colors

you can't see. As far as odors, well, we in
the hive tend to laugh at your abilities.

So that's it! You came to put me down!

Of course not! I came to enjoy the pool,
the flowers, the trees ... but since we're talking,
will you stop using those foolish clichés about
bees? I often relax a whole night here
and catch a nap before dawn.

Do you? I didn't realize. I'm sorry, Bee, I ...

And stop making so much about the dance
we do in the hive! Infinite dissertations!
As if your noisy jerking about in a boxy room
isn't the same: messages passing back and forth.

You're right, Bee, now that I think of it, I'll ...

But she was finished. She flew a few loops for my
enjoyment, then weaved away to visit the garden
before the morning sun hived the stars. At home
I thought of all the bee had said. I closed my eyes
and wandered once again through cycads and ferns,
blue and tropical gardens, fountains and pools,
realizing now what is owned and what is not.

Acknowledgements

Thank you to artist Penelope Stewart for soliciting poems for *Chasing Daphne: A beeswax architectural intervention, Lotusland, Montecito, California* (The Tree Museum, 2014). The following poems appeared in her catalog and are reprinted here with permission:

Ron Alexander: "Distress Signal"
Diane August: "Nectar Like Chocolate"
Gudrun Bortman: "Room of Wax"
Laure-Anne Bosselaar: "Pantoum from the Wax-Tiled Room"
Mary Brown: "Of Honey" and "¹wax \'waks\n"
Tessa Flanagan: "The Humming"
Suzanne Frost: "Lea and the Sound of Bees"
Luci Janssen: "Beescape"
Richard Jarrette: "The Godot Tree"
Chryss Yost: "Wicked"

In addition, the following poems have been previously published or are forthcoming as noted and are included here with the permission of the poet:

Paul Fericano: "Song of the Beeswax" was first published in *The French Literary Review*, October 2013 (Paris).
Richard Jarrette: "Honey for the Women" first appeared in Green Writers Press "Zine" (November, 2014). "Honey for the Women" and "The Godot Tree" will be included in the forthcoming *A Hundred Million Years of Nectar Dances* (Green Writers Press, 2015).
Gabriella Klein, "The Honeycomb Conjecture" in *Land Sparing* (Nightboat Books, 2015)
Paul J. Willis, "Extra Innings" in *Visiting Home* (Pecan Grove Press, 2008)
Chryss Yost, "Wicked" in *Mouth & Fruit* (Gunpowder Press, 2014)

Thanks also to the Santa Barbara Arts Commission and the City for their support of the position of Poet Laureate. Finally, thank you to all the poets for their contributions to this project.

About the Editors

Nancy Gifford is an artist and curator who worked in Los Angeles till the early 90's then moved to London and spent the next ten years in England, France, and Florida. She sat on the Patron Board of MOCA in Miami and owned Wynwood Contemporary. She was a founding member of the now burgeoning Wynwood Art District. In 2008 Nancy moved to Montecito, California. She sits on the board of the Museum of Contemporary Art Santa Barbara and is a member of the Westmont Museum Arts Council and founding member of the Museum Contemporaries of the Santa Barbara Museum of Art. She also sits on the board of the Arts Fund Santa Barbara and is head of their community gallery program.

Nancy has curated numerous exhibitions including SWARM at the Pavilion Gallery at Ganna Walska Lotusland. She continues to exhibit her own art widely, most recently as part of *Requiem for the Bibliophile* at the Museum of Contemporary Art Santa Barbara.

Chryss Yost was appointed Santa Barbara Poet Laureate in 2013. Her first full-length book of poems, *Mouth & Fruit*, was published in April 2014 by Gunpowder Press. She is co-editor, with Dana Gioia and Jack Hicks, of *California Poetry, from the Gold Rush to the Present* (Heyday, 2004). She is also co-editor, with Don Selby and Diane Boller, of *Poetry Daily, a Year of Poems from the World's Most Popular Poetry Web Site* (Sourcebooks, 2004). She was the long-time managing editor for the *Journal of Haitian Studies* and currently works with international students at UCSB. A native of San Diego, she has lived in Santa Barbara since 1990, where she has been a poetic collaborator and organizer for many years. She teaches poetry at the Santa Barbara Music and Arts Conservatory.

Chryss lives with her husband, George Yatchisin, and their assortment of dogs and chickens. Her daughter, Cassidy, lives in Australia.

www.ingramcontent.com/pod-product-compliance
Lightning Source LLC
Chambersburg PA
CBHW032047290426
44110CB00012B/994